MW00438856

# PISCES

## A GUIDED JOURNAL

### Constance Stellas

**ADAMS MEDIA**
New York London Toronto Sydney New Delhi

Adams Media
An Imprint of Simon & Schuster, Inc.
100 Technology Center Drive
Stoughton, Massachusetts 02072

First Adams Media hardcover edition September 2022

ADAMS MEDIA and colophon are trademarks of Simon & Schuster.

For information about special discounts for bulk purchases, please contact Simon & Schuster Special Sales at 1-866-506-1949 or business@simonandschuster.com.

The Simon & Schuster Speakers Bureau can bring authors to your live event. For more information or to book an event contact the Simon & Schuster Speakers Bureau at 1-866-248-3049 or visit our website at www.simonspeakers.com.

Interior design by Colleen Cunningham
Interior illustrations by Tess Armstrong
Interior images © Getty Images/Vikiss, Mara Fribus; Simon & Schuster, Inc.

Manufactured in China

10 9 8 7 6 5 4 3 2 1

ISBN 978-1-5072-1954-6

# CONTENTS

# INTRODUCTION

**Are you interested in how the stars may influence your characteristics?** Wanting a little celestial insight into how you can strengthen your relationships? Looking for guidance in using your innate intuition to achieve your goals? Guided journaling can be a dialogue between your thoughts, feelings, and aspects of your sign and element. By reflecting in an intentional way, you can begin to understand yourself—and how you interact with the world around you—better.

A water sign, Pisces is artistic, mystical, and compassionate. She prefers to live in a flowing, idealistic, and easygoing world without strife. Are there times when your intuition pulls you in a certain direction? Or when your dreams seem to be telling you something important? The prompts in this book will allow you to follow your intuition with more confidence and understand your dreams by exploring your Pisces tendencies and what you may share with other water signs.

Journaling can also help you protect your sensitivities and share your imaginative world. Pisces' symbol is two fish tied together by a silken cord: One fish dreams in the depths of the ocean; the other fish reaches above the sea, looking to thrive on the earth. They represent the Piscean energy that exists between heaven and earth. There is a conflict between these two realms: Do you often have a desire to retreat from the world? By reflecting on the prompts in this book, you'll gain a deeper understanding of what has and hasn't helped you deal with concrete realities and learn how to create a more viable future in line with your dreams.

When you write, you connect with your feelings, desires, and everything in between. And when prompts drive you to contemplate the wealth of astrological wisdom that each element and Sun sign offers, it can lead to surprising, creative insights. You may have recognized your need for music to change your mood but didn't realize that this tendency can also help you retreat when you feel frazzled. Or perhaps you never considered the importance of calming quality time with pets. This book will help you explore yourself and your place among the stars.

# HOW TO USE THIS BOOK

**Welcome to your astrology journal!** This guided journal is divided into three parts to help you explore your connections to the stars.

## PART ONE

First, there are prompts about astrology in general, from how you feel about astrological wisdom to what you notice about your relationships with different signs and your experiences with reading horoscopes. The long and rich history of astrology can truly enhance your life and deepen your self-knowledge. Whatever strikes your fancy is a prompt to pursue! The purpose is not to master celestial knowledge but to turn your thoughts to the cosmos and reflect in an intentional way that may uncover some surprising insights.

## PART TWO

The second part features prompts about your element. In astrology, there are four elements:

- Fire
- Earth
- Air
- Water

There are three zodiac signs in each element.

THE
PASSIONATE
FIRE SIGNS
ARE:

**ARIES**

**LEO**

**SAGITTARIUS**

---

THE
PRACTICAL
EARTH SIGNS
ARE:

**TAURUS**

**VIRGO**

**CAPRICORN**

---

THE
COMMUNICATIVE
AIR SIGNS
ARE:

**GEMINI**

**LIBRA**

**AQUARIUS**

---

THE
EMOTIONAL
WATER SIGNS
ARE:

**CANCER**

**SCORPIO**

**PISCES**

All members of the same element have an affinity; being with your elemental brothers or sisters can often feel comfortable because they speak your language. Understanding the characteristics of your element can give insight into good health practices and ways to relax and recharge, as well as how you might approach aspects of life such as work and relationships.

## PART THREE

Finally, the third part of this journal concentrates on your Sun sign. This is the position of the sun when you were born. The Sun sign is a dominant feature in a person's entire chart. It reveals your:

- Psychological characteristics
- Health habits
- Relationship affinities
- Spiritual mission in this lifetime

Each Sun sign also has a ruling planet that gives the sign a certain kind of energy; a symbol that represents the characteristics of the sign's personality; and a modality that reveals whether that sign charges ahead in life, prefers the security of things remaining the same, or is open to the changes that come along. Consider these prompts intuitively. When something speaks to you and you think "Yes! That's me," reflect on the questions and any suggestions posed by the prompt. If you don't feel particularly drawn to a prompt, you may want to return to it later. If the information or questions in a prompt make you feel uncomfortable, consider whether there is something hidden or suppressed in your life that it awakens. Or you may use the page to explore why this doesn't fit you. True, not every aspect of the Sun sign will resonate with every person, so you may want to look at your full birth chart to help color the portrait of you that you create in this journal.

Astrology has become more and more popular, thanks to the ease of calculating birth charts online; the availability of daily, weekly, or monthly horoscopes delivered straight to your inbox; popular lists of famous people according to their Sun signs; and more. Ancient astrologers may have appreciated these options, *but* a computer is not a person, and the information that computer printouts offer is standard. Anyone born on the same day, time, year, and place as you would have the same astrology chart; however, people are individuals. There's a lot more to you than what is written about a Sun sign or astrological element. The beauty of this journal is that you can reflect on what astrology means to *you* and understand the nuances of your sign and element and how they do or don't relate to you as a unique person. Use this journal as your guide in exploring what the stars can teach you about yourself!

Astrology is the study of star and planetary patterns and what they mean for individuals and societies. Observing the regular motions of the sun, the moon, and other planets, ancient people became adept at interpreting what these celestial bodies and cycles meant. Today, there is a new renaissance in astrology, thanks to the Internet. Now anyone can find out the locations of the sun, the moon, Venus, and more at the time of their birth in just seconds, and subscribe to a service featuring daily, weekly, and monthly astrological forecasts. Consulting astrologers also offer star wisdom for health, business dealings, romance, spiritual development, and marriage.

In this part, you'll find thought-provoking prompts to guide you in reflecting on astrology in a more general context, rather than focusing on one specific sign or element. The sun, the moon, Mercury, Venus, Mars, Jupiter, Saturn, Uranus, Neptune, and Pluto: All of these celestial energies make up a natal chart and become a blueprint for gaining deeper self-knowledge and guiding your life. You can explore the astrological patterns in your family, track how different events like eclipses and equinoxes impact your mood and experiences, consider your beliefs on fate versus free will, and more. Enjoy this journey into the cosmos.

# PART ONE

# GETTING TO KNOW THE WORLD OF ASTROLOGY

Imagine you are lying on the grass or a beach or sitting on a bench at night. You can see the stars, perhaps the moon. Depending on the time of year, you might even see Venus twinkling on the horizon or a distant red glow from Mars. Describe what you feel. Awe? Like you are part of the universe? Or like you are insignificant compared to the vast celestial sky? Maybe curious to know more about the heavens?

If you were an ancient navigator and only had the constellations and the moon with which to navigate your ship to get home, would you feel comforted by the regularity of the patterns in the night sky? Write about a time when you felt lost literally or emotionally. Did the moon or a twinkling star give you courage? Did you notice if the moon during that time was just a crescent or full? Or maybe it was somewhere in between?

Astrology has become more and more popular in recent years, thanks to the Internet! Do you believe that everything astrology says about your sign is true? Write about a positive experience you have had reading your horoscope. Did you follow the advice? What happened?

........................................................................................................
........................................................................................................
........................................................................................................
........................................................................................................
........................................................................................................
........................................................................................................
........................................................................................................
........................................................................................................
........................................................................................................
........................................................................................................
........................................................................................................
........................................................................................................
........................................................................................................
........................................................................................................
........................................................................................................
........................................................................................................
........................................................................................................
........................................................................................................
........................................................................................................
........................................................................................................
........................................................................................................
........................................................................................................
........................................................................................................
........................................................................................................

What charms you about astrology? What bothers or concerns you about it? Are you mindful of the monthly zodiac sign changes? Describe any feelings you have about how certain zodiac time periods affect you. For example, in spring, when the sun is in Aries, maybe you feel energized.

Are there certain signs with which you are more harmonious? Less harmonious? Write about your experiences.

........................................................................................................
........................................................................................................
........................................................................................................
........................................................................................................
........................................................................................................
........................................................................................................
........................................................................................................
........................................................................................................
........................................................................................................
........................................................................................................
........................................................................................................
........................................................................................................
........................................................................................................
........................................................................................................
........................................................................................................
........................................................................................................
........................................................................................................
........................................................................................................
........................................................................................................
........................................................................................................
........................................................................................................
........................................................................................................
........................................................................................................
........................................................................................................
........................................................................................................
........................................................................................................
........................................................................................................
........................................................................................................

A person's fate or destiny is a lifelong path. Describe how you feel when you read an astrological prediction for your future. Do you think it is good to know this information? Or better not to know? Do you use this information, keep it in mind, or ignore it?

..................................................................................................
..................................................................................................
..................................................................................................
..................................................................................................
..................................................................................................
..................................................................................................
..................................................................................................
..................................................................................................
..................................................................................................
..................................................................................................
..................................................................................................
..................................................................................................
..................................................................................................
..................................................................................................
..................................................................................................
..................................................................................................
..................................................................................................
..................................................................................................
..................................................................................................
..................................................................................................
..................................................................................................
..................................................................................................
..................................................................................................
..................................................................................................

Each zodiac sign is ruled by a planet or by the Sun or the Moon. Do you identify with Mercury, Venus, Mars, Jupiter, Saturn, Uranus, Neptune, Pluto, the Sun, or the Moon? Is it the planet your sign is ruled by? If not, describe your feelings about your own sign's planet. Do you think knowing more about your planet brings you insights into your personality or fortune?

......................................................................................................
......................................................................................................
......................................................................................................
......................................................................................................
......................................................................................................
......................................................................................................
......................................................................................................
......................................................................................................
......................................................................................................
......................................................................................................
......................................................................................................
......................................................................................................
......................................................................................................
......................................................................................................
......................................................................................................
......................................................................................................
......................................................................................................
......................................................................................................
......................................................................................................
......................................................................................................
......................................................................................................
......................................................................................................

The most famous—or infamous!—astrological event is Mercury Retrograde. This happens three times each year and means that Mercury appears to be moving backward in relation to the earth's orbit. It is common during these periods to experience electronic mishaps, communications going awry, and difficulties and delays in scheduling. Describe any Mercury Retrograde experiences you may have noticed. Were you forced to be more patient than usual?

If your Sun is in Gemini or Virgo, both signs ruled by Mercury, you may experience more personal confusion during Mercury in retrograde. Describe any personal confusion that you or your Gemini or Virgo friends experience at this time. Did you notice that you or they felt relief when Mercury was no longer retrograde?

......................................................................................................................
......................................................................................................................
......................................................................................................................
......................................................................................................................
......................................................................................................................
......................................................................................................................
......................................................................................................................
......................................................................................................................
......................................................................................................................
......................................................................................................................
......................................................................................................................
......................................................................................................................
......................................................................................................................
......................................................................................................................
......................................................................................................................
......................................................................................................................
......................................................................................................................
......................................................................................................................
......................................................................................................................
......................................................................................................................
......................................................................................................................
......................................................................................................................
......................................................................................................................
......................................................................................................................

The moon is our closest celestial neighbor, and its rhythms influence daily life. The monthly new moon marks the beginning of the moon's phases. At the new moon, people make wishes or set intentions with support from the moon's increasing energy as she waxes toward the full moon (the peak of lunar energy). Do you tend to notice the moon's phase, influence, or sign? Write about your relationship with and feeling toward this light.

..................................................................................................
..................................................................................................
..................................................................................................
..................................................................................................
..................................................................................................
..................................................................................................
..................................................................................................
..................................................................................................
..................................................................................................
..................................................................................................
..................................................................................................
..................................................................................................
..................................................................................................
..................................................................................................
..................................................................................................
..................................................................................................
..................................................................................................
..................................................................................................
..................................................................................................
..................................................................................................
..................................................................................................

Many astrologers believe that a person's chart can indicate past lives. What historical time period do you feel connected to? Who do you feel you might have been in a past life? What was your profession? Do you believe a past life can influence your present life? If so, how?

Each astrological sign is either masculine or feminine. This designation has nothing to do with gender or sexual orientation. The masculine signs radiate outwardly, and the feminine signs inwardly. Make a list of all the signs in your birth chart. Which energy dominates? Or perhaps they are equal? Do you feel these descriptions are true to your self-image?

.........................................................................................
.........................................................................................
.........................................................................................
.........................................................................................
.........................................................................................
.........................................................................................
.........................................................................................
.........................................................................................
.........................................................................................
.........................................................................................
.........................................................................................
.........................................................................................
.........................................................................................
.........................................................................................
.........................................................................................
.........................................................................................
.........................................................................................
.........................................................................................
.........................................................................................
.........................................................................................
.........................................................................................
.........................................................................................
.........................................................................................
.........................................................................................
.........................................................................................
.........................................................................................
.........................................................................................
.........................................................................................
.........................................................................................
.........................................................................................
.........................................................................................
.........................................................................................

In astrology, each sign has a symbol associated with it. Think about the symbol for your sign. Explore your feelings toward this symbol. Do any of its characteristics apply to you? You might write a story about yourself and what your symbol means to you. For example, as a Leo, are you more like a roaring lion or a purring cat?

As you will discover in this guided journey, there are four elements: fire, earth, air, and water. Each sign belongs to one element. Have you noticed that the signs of people you get along with have the same element as you do? Or a certain different element? Write about your experiences with people of the same and different elements.

Some people believe that following astrology curtails free will by forecasting the future. Do you believe this? Do you think it is possible that by knowing about your sign and using the stars as guides for the future you can make better choices in your life? Or do you feel controlled by what the stars say? Reflect on your feelings about free will and the stars.

...............................................................................................................
...............................................................................................................
...............................................................................................................
...............................................................................................................
...............................................................................................................
...............................................................................................................
...............................................................................................................
...............................................................................................................
...............................................................................................................
...............................................................................................................
...............................................................................................................
...............................................................................................................
...............................................................................................................
...............................................................................................................
...............................................................................................................
...............................................................................................................
...............................................................................................................
...............................................................................................................
...............................................................................................................
...............................................................................................................
...............................................................................................................
...............................................................................................................
...............................................................................................................

Throughout the history of astrology, healers and physicians were required to study the positions of the planets in order to help their patients. They believed that the planetary energies could help or hinder healing the soul and body. What do you think about this idea? Can you implement any of your astrological insights into your health practices?

........................................................................................
........................................................................................
........................................................................................
........................................................................................
........................................................................................
........................................................................................
........................................................................................
........................................................................................
........................................................................................
........................................................................................
........................................................................................
........................................................................................
........................................................................................
........................................................................................
........................................................................................
........................................................................................
........................................................................................
........................................................................................
........................................................................................
........................................................................................
........................................................................................
........................................................................................
........................................................................................

The position of the sun, the moon, and the ascendant are the three most important placements in a person's natal chart. If you know your birth time, you can easily determine these with the help of an app or astrology website. Explore your astrological trio and write down your feelings about these placements. Do you feel more connected to your moon or to your ascendant? Are there any patterns you notice, like the same element for each placement?

Eclipses were awesome phenomena for the ancients—and still have us in awe today! In a total solar eclipse, the sun's light is blocked by the moon, and the atmosphere darkens. In a lunar eclipse, the moon is blocked by the earth, and we cannot see this silvery orb. Most years have four eclipses. Do you pay attention to this heavenly event? Do you notice any patterns, either within yourself or in your surroundings during an eclipse? Research when the next eclipse will be, and record your feelings for the week leading up to the event.

How do you typically "use" astrology? Do you find it useful for self-understanding? Understanding other people? Exploring your friendships and/or partnerships? Do daily horoscopes guide your actions? Or do you see astrology as more of a guide for larger focuses in life? Write about an experience when an astrological tip helped you in some way.

....................................................................................................

....................................................................................................

....................................................................................................

....................................................................................................

....................................................................................................

....................................................................................................

....................................................................................................

....................................................................................................

....................................................................................................

....................................................................................................

....................................................................................................

....................................................................................................

....................................................................................................

....................................................................................................

....................................................................................................

....................................................................................................

....................................................................................................

....................................................................................................

....................................................................................................

....................................................................................................

....................................................................................................

....................................................................................................

Have you noticed that people in the same family often have the same signs? Or that other positions in their charts correspond? It's frequently the case! Take a look at your family's and extended family's signs, and reflect on the similarities and differences.

....................................................................................................
....................................................................................................
....................................................................................................
....................................................................................................
....................................................................................................
....................................................................................................
....................................................................................................
....................................................................................................
....................................................................................................
....................................................................................................
....................................................................................................
....................................................................................................
....................................................................................................
....................................................................................................
....................................................................................................
....................................................................................................
....................................................................................................
....................................................................................................
....................................................................................................
....................................................................................................
....................................................................................................
....................................................................................................
....................................................................................................
....................................................................................................

Saturn is the farthest planet you can see with the naked eye. It rules time, structure, and lessons of life. A major astrological transit is the Saturn Return, when Saturn returns to its natal chart position. This happens between ages twenty-eight and thirty. Where is Saturn in your chart? Have you experienced this return? Whether you have experienced your Saturn Return or not, write about your feelings toward the current path of your life, relationships, health, and spiritual development. If you have experienced your Saturn Return, how did your life look during these years?

Aside from your Saturn Return, another important transit (when a planet returns to its original position in your birth chart) is with the planet Jupiter. Jupiter is called the benefic of the zodiac. He helps us feel generous toward ourselves and others, is good for business, and can bring new areas of creativity into life. Jupiter returns to his birthplace every twelve years. Think about your birthday years at each twelfth year so far. Write about your feelings and activities in those years. Were the experiences positive? Expansive? Creative?

......................................................................................................
......................................................................................................
......................................................................................................
......................................................................................................
......................................................................................................
......................................................................................................
......................................................................................................
......................................................................................................
......................................................................................................
......................................................................................................
......................................................................................................
......................................................................................................
......................................................................................................
......................................................................................................
......................................................................................................
......................................................................................................
......................................................................................................
......................................................................................................
......................................................................................................
......................................................................................................

The solstices, summer and winter, occur at opposite signs: Cancer in the summer, and Capricorn in the winter. They mark the height of sunlight in summer and the depths of darkness in winter. How is your mood at these times? Describe how these essential astrological markers affect you.

........................................................................................
........................................................................................
........................................................................................
........................................................................................
........................................................................................
........................................................................................
........................................................................................
........................................................................................
........................................................................................
........................................................................................
........................................................................................
........................................................................................
........................................................................................
........................................................................................
........................................................................................
........................................................................................
........................................................................................
........................................................................................
........................................................................................
........................................................................................
........................................................................................
........................................................................................
........................................................................................
........................................................................................
........................................................................................
........................................................................................

Two major points in nature and the celestial calendar are the equinoxes: the fall equinox (Libra) and the spring equinox (Aries). These events mean there is equal daylight and darkness during that day. Do you have any particular feelings during these times of the year? Happy fall is coming after a hot summer? Or anticipating spring after a harsh winter? Write your feelings about the rhythm of nature and how it corresponds to your experience of the seasons. If you live in the southern hemisphere, the equinoxes are reversed.

........................................................................................
........................................................................................
........................................................................................
........................................................................................
........................................................................................
........................................................................................
........................................................................................
........................................................................................
........................................................................................
........................................................................................
........................................................................................
........................................................................................
........................................................................................
........................................................................................
........................................................................................
........................................................................................
........................................................................................
........................................................................................
........................................................................................
........................................................................................
........................................................................................

If someone you know says, "I don't believe in astrology, it's rubbish," what do you say back? Write a dialogue between you and a skeptical person. What are your points of agreement? Of disagreement?

......................................................................................................
......................................................................................................
......................................................................................................
......................................................................................................
......................................................................................................
......................................................................................................
......................................................................................................
......................................................................................................
......................................................................................................
......................................................................................................
......................................................................................................
......................................................................................................
......................................................................................................
......................................................................................................
......................................................................................................
......................................................................................................
......................................................................................................
......................................................................................................
......................................................................................................
......................................................................................................
......................................................................................................
......................................................................................................
......................................................................................................
......................................................................................................

Have you ever noticed that some days feel lucky and positive and that during other days nothing seems to go right? It could be that the planetary pattern in the sky is not in harmony with your personal planets! Keep a record of good and bad days and the placements of the planets during each day. Reflect on any patterns. (You can find the daily position of the planets online.)

Throughout history, people have sought to understand the world around them. Today we have scientific equipment to inform us of the makeup of the universe, but ancient peoples could only observe the basic elements that they saw in their lives: fire, earth, air, and water. They associated each of these elements with an astrological sign and certain characteristics, and physicians used these characteristics to treat and heal their patients. The elements and their characteristics are:

**FIRE** (Aries, Leo, Sagittarius): Fire signs are known for their passionate energy and impetuosity. They often need to moderate their bursts of enthusiasm to prevent burnout.

**EARTH** (Taurus, Virgo, Capricorn): Earth signs are practical, cautious, and seek out security with a measured pace. Cultivating change and taking a few risks can enhance their lives, boost their health, and encourage flexibility.

**AIR** (Gemini, Libra, Aquarius): Air signs are changeable and mentally oriented; they enjoy living in creative possibilities and have highly sensitive nervous systems. Getting "down to earth" can help air signs move forward realistically.

**WATER** (Cancer, Scorpio, Pisces): Water is the element of feelings, and all water signs react to life emotionally. Calming their waves of emotion in order to see a situation clearly is a lifelong challenge for all water signs.

The more than two dozen prompts in this part of the book will give you a platform for understanding more about yourself and your nature based on your element.

# PART TWO
# GETTING TO KNOW YOUR ELEMENT

Water is the element of emotions: your own personal tides. For one day, write about your feelings, hour by hour, or perhaps even minute by minute. Are you amazed at how your own "tides" change?

.......................................................................................................................
.......................................................................................................................
.......................................................................................................................
.......................................................................................................................
.......................................................................................................................
.......................................................................................................................
.......................................................................................................................
.......................................................................................................................
.......................................................................................................................
.......................................................................................................................
.......................................................................................................................
.......................................................................................................................
.......................................................................................................................
.......................................................................................................................
.......................................................................................................................
.......................................................................................................................
.......................................................................................................................
.......................................................................................................................
.......................................................................................................................
.......................................................................................................................
.......................................................................................................................
.......................................................................................................................
.......................................................................................................................
.......................................................................................................................
.......................................................................................................................
.......................................................................................................................

Water can cleanse our minds as well as our bodies. Do you take a shower or bath before sleeping? Or in the morning before starting your day? Try both, and write about which soothes you and which peps you up.

......................................................................................
......................................................................................
......................................................................................
......................................................................................
......................................................................................
......................................................................................
......................................................................................
......................................................................................
......................................................................................
......................................................................................
......................................................................................
......................................................................................
......................................................................................
......................................................................................
......................................................................................
......................................................................................
......................................................................................
......................................................................................
......................................................................................
......................................................................................
......................................................................................
......................................................................................
......................................................................................

........................................................................................
........................................................................................
........................................................................................
........................................................................................
........................................................................................
........................................................................................
........................................................................................
........................................................................................
........................................................................................
........................................................................................
........................................................................................
........................................................................................
........................................................................................
........................................................................................
........................................................................................
........................................................................................
........................................................................................
........................................................................................
........................................................................................
........................................................................................
........................................................................................
........................................................................................
........................................................................................
........................................................................................
........................................................................................
........................................................................................
........................................................................................
........................................................................................

When a person is a water sign and has lots of water signs in their chart, they usually *feel* more than *think*. Notice how often you begin a conversation with phrases like "I feel." Can you distinguish the difference between what you feel and what you think? What topics bring up the strongest feelings for you?

........................................................................................................

........................................................................................................

........................................................................................................

........................................................................................................

........................................................................................................

........................................................................................................

........................................................................................................

........................................................................................................

........................................................................................................

........................................................................................................

........................................................................................................

........................................................................................................

........................................................................................................

........................................................................................................

........................................................................................................

........................................................................................................

........................................................................................................

........................................................................................................

........................................................................................................

........................................................................................................

........................................................................................................

........................................................................................................

Which type of water attracts you the most: a pool, ocean, lake, or pond? What about a calm sea versus heavy surf? Which kind of water do you feel typifies your sign?

........................................................................................................
........................................................................................................
........................................................................................................
........................................................................................................
........................................................................................................
........................................................................................................
........................................................................................................
........................................................................................................
........................................................................................................
........................................................................................................
........................................................................................................
........................................................................................................
........................................................................................................
........................................................................................................
........................................................................................................
........................................................................................................
........................................................................................................
........................................................................................................
........................................................................................................
........................................................................................................
........................................................................................................
........................................................................................................
........................................................................................................
........................................................................................................
........................................................................................................
........................................................................................................

Water has the power to heal—and, like in a flood, tsunami, or hurricane, to be destructive. Which aspects of water have you experienced? Write about your favorite *and* least favorite experiences with water. How did they affect your feelings toward the power of water?

........................................................................................
........................................................................................
........................................................................................
........................................................................................
........................................................................................
........................................................................................
........................................................................................
........................................................................................
........................................................................................
........................................................................................
........................................................................................
........................................................................................
........................................................................................
........................................................................................
........................................................................................
........................................................................................
........................................................................................
........................................................................................
........................................................................................
........................................................................................
........................................................................................
........................................................................................
........................................................................................
........................................................................................

The Moon, ruler of water sign Cancer, governs all the tides of the oceans and other large bodies of water on Earth. As a water sign, do you feel that you have personal high and low tides? Do you feel they are passing moods and have confidence that they will change? Or do you often feel stuck in stormy seas? Explore the easy or difficult flow of your personal tides.

........................................................................................................

........................................................................................................

........................................................................................................

........................................................................................................

........................................................................................................

........................................................................................................

........................................................................................................

........................................................................................................

........................................................................................................

........................................................................................................

........................................................................................................

........................................................................................................

........................................................................................................

........................................................................................................

........................................................................................................

........................................................................................................

........................................................................................................

........................................................................................................

........................................................................................................

........................................................................................................

........................................................................................................

........................................................................................................

Drinking water is important for health, and the water signs particularly need to keep hydrated! Amid the innumerable products of water: bubbly, still water, coconut water, electrolyte water, flavored water, or sugary soda, which do you prefer to drink? Do you notice different feelings according to your water intake? Reflect on the best experience you have had drinking a refreshing glass of water.

.............................................................................................
.............................................................................................
.............................................................................................
.............................................................................................
.............................................................................................
.............................................................................................
.............................................................................................
.............................................................................................
.............................................................................................
.............................................................................................
.............................................................................................
.............................................................................................
.............................................................................................
.............................................................................................
.............................................................................................
.............................................................................................
.............................................................................................
.............................................................................................
.............................................................................................
.............................................................................................
.............................................................................................

Water signs in astrology have "yin" energy. "Yin" is a Chinese term referring to energy that is expressed inwardly. Yin signs draw other people and experiences to them. Do you recognize this trait in yourself? Write about a time when your feelings brought you a wonderful or surprising experience.

Water is the element of feelings. Write about an experience when you became entangled with your feelings and were so emotional that you couldn't see reason. What happened?

Crying is the body's way of releasing different feelings. Emotional water signs can be especially prone to this form of release. Do you cry easily? What situations provoke tears of joy, sadness, anger, or grief?

..........................................................................................................
..........................................................................................................
..........................................................................................................
..........................................................................................................
..........................................................................................................
..........................................................................................................
..........................................................................................................
..........................................................................................................
..........................................................................................................
..........................................................................................................
..........................................................................................................
..........................................................................................................
..........................................................................................................
..........................................................................................................
..........................................................................................................
..........................................................................................................
..........................................................................................................
..........................................................................................................
..........................................................................................................
..........................................................................................................
..........................................................................................................
..........................................................................................................
..........................................................................................................
..........................................................................................................

Many counselors tell clients that they must "calm down" when dealing with emotional issues. A more relaxed state of mind helps you address the issue at hand from a rational place. But water signs, especially Scorpio, have a hard time calming down when their feelings are flowing. Has this happened to you? What were the circumstances, and how did the situation resolve? For water signs, sometimes "waiting until it passes" is the best way to calm down.

.................................................................................
.................................................................................
.................................................................................
.................................................................................
.................................................................................
.................................................................................
.................................................................................
.................................................................................
.................................................................................
.................................................................................
.................................................................................
.................................................................................
.................................................................................
.................................................................................
.................................................................................
.................................................................................
.................................................................................
.................................................................................
.................................................................................
.................................................................................
.................................................................................
.................................................................................

Do you ever have dreams filled with water? This could be a puddle or a huge wave. Sometimes water dreams signify fear, particularly fear of a new feeling or experience. Write about a dream where the element water was a main character. What was the dream about, and how did you feel when you woke up?

Water signs often feel at home when they can see water outside their window. Do you feel more comfortable on the coasts of the US or your country, near the ocean, in the desert, along a lake or pond, or in the plains? Write about your experience living in different environments. How does each environment make you feel?

........................................................................................

........................................................................................

........................................................................................

........................................................................................

........................................................................................

........................................................................................

........................................................................................

........................................................................................

........................................................................................

........................................................................................

........................................................................................

........................................................................................

........................................................................................

........................................................................................

........................................................................................

........................................................................................

........................................................................................

........................................................................................

........................................................................................

........................................................................................

........................................................................................

........................................................................................

........................................................................................

........................................................................................

As the feeling signs of the zodiac, water signs are often frustrated with this increasingly computerized world. Computers can't feel—they only provoke feelings in users, and often the feeling is irritation. Write about your feelings toward your devices. Do they serve you or frustrate you more?

..................................................................................................
..................................................................................................
..................................................................................................
..................................................................................................
..................................................................................................
..................................................................................................
..................................................................................................
..................................................................................................
..................................................................................................
..................................................................................................
..................................................................................................
..................................................................................................
..................................................................................................
..................................................................................................
..................................................................................................
..................................................................................................
..................................................................................................
..................................................................................................
..................................................................................................
..................................................................................................
..................................................................................................
..................................................................................................
..................................................................................................
..................................................................................................

In relationships, water signs need emotional closeness and partners with whom they can express their deepest feelings. Write about the element compatibility you have with your significant other or a close friend. Are you both water signs? If not, what signs do you have (or have previously had) relationships with? Which element combo(s) works the best for you?

........................................................................................
........................................................................................
........................................................................................
........................................................................................
........................................................................................
........................................................................................
........................................................................................
........................................................................................
........................................................................................
........................................................................................
........................................................................................
........................................................................................
........................................................................................
........................................................................................
........................................................................................
........................................................................................
........................................................................................
........................................................................................
........................................................................................
........................................................................................
........................................................................................
........................................................................................

Do you like to swim? Or prefer to be on the water in a boat? Sometimes being immersed in water is not comfortable for water element signs. They can feel afraid or overwhelmed. Write about your feelings toward different water activities.

........................................................................................
........................................................................................
........................................................................................
........................................................................................
........................................................................................
........................................................................................
........................................................................................
........................................................................................
........................................................................................
........................................................................................
........................................................................................
........................................................................................
........................................................................................
........................................................................................
........................................................................................
........................................................................................
........................................................................................
........................................................................................
........................................................................................
........................................................................................
........................................................................................
........................................................................................
........................................................................................
........................................................................................

Water signs, especially Cancer, tend to stay close to home. They enjoy the protection of a familiar environment. Does this describe you? Write about how you feel about your home, as well as what kind of temporary home you need or like when traveling. RVs could be a favorite. Or you may prefer a cozy cabin over a tent.

Water is the element of instincts. You tend to follow your instincts about an opportunity or a person—and usually, you are right! Write about a time when your instincts led you to a good experience, as well as a time when your instincts warned you to stay away but you didn't listen.

........................................................................................
........................................................................................
........................................................................................
........................................................................................
........................................................................................
........................................................................................
........................................................................................
........................................................................................
........................................................................................
........................................................................................
........................................................................................
........................................................................................
........................................................................................
........................................................................................
........................................................................................
........................................................................................
........................................................................................
........................................................................................
........................................................................................
........................................................................................
........................................................................................
........................................................................................
........................................................................................
........................................................................................

As a water sign, you may be both an introvert and an extrovert. Write about the times when you favor company and times when you want to be alone. How do these changing moods work for you?

...........................................................................................................

...........................................................................................................

...........................................................................................................

...........................................................................................................

...........................................................................................................

...........................................................................................................

...........................................................................................................

...........................................................................................................

...........................................................................................................

...........................................................................................................

...........................................................................................................

...........................................................................................................

...........................................................................................................

...........................................................................................................

...........................................................................................................

...........................................................................................................

...........................................................................................................

...........................................................................................................

...........................................................................................................

...........................................................................................................

...........................................................................................................

...........................................................................................................

...........................................................................................................

...........................................................................................................

Waterfalls are cleansing for body and mind. Do you have a favorite waterfall that you visit or know of? The next time you are stressed, try meditating on that place, envisioning the rush of the water or the gentle flow of a smaller waterfall. How did you feel before and after this meditation?

........................................................................................

........................................................................................

........................................................................................

........................................................................................

........................................................................................

........................................................................................

........................................................................................

........................................................................................

........................................................................................

........................................................................................

........................................................................................

........................................................................................

........................................................................................

........................................................................................

........................................................................................

........................................................................................

........................................................................................

........................................................................................

........................................................................................

........................................................................................

........................................................................................

........................................................................................

........................................................................................

........................................................................................

When you were a child, did you have a favorite water place: a rain pipe, a trickle down the street of your childhood home, a babbling brook, a puddle, or a small pond? Describe the place and the feelings you remember from that time. Water is the element of memory as well as emotions. And all water signs have deep feelings about their memories.

........................................................................................
........................................................................................
........................................................................................
........................................................................................
........................................................................................
........................................................................................
........................................................................................
........................................................................................
........................................................................................
........................................................................................
........................................................................................
........................................................................................
........................................................................................
........................................................................................
........................................................................................
........................................................................................
........................................................................................
........................................................................................
........................................................................................
........................................................................................
........................................................................................
........................................................................................

Water signs are usually talented in visual arts, especially painting. Painting with watercolors is a beautiful combination of artistic expression and your prime element. Do you paint? If so, reflect on your feelings about both painting and watercolors. If you haven't tried painting, consider studying or working with a painting kit to start your watercolor journey, and reflect on your feelings along the way.

Different historical eras usually fascinate water signs. The flow of history is like a river of life and experience. If you could live in a different historical era, what would it be? What would you do?

Do you like crowds? Most water signs prefer smaller groups where they can relax. Crowds are full of alien feelings for water signs. Describe your feelings when you are in a large crowd versus a smaller gathering.

Do you prefer a cloudy, rainy day or bright sunshine? Many water signs are very sensitive to the sun; they tend to prefer clouds and love to listen to the sound of rain. Describe your favorite weather and how you feel when it rains or snows. Where do you most like to be during cloudy weather?

Many musicians are water signs. They have a natural sense of rhythm and melody! Are you musical? If so, what instrument do you play? Do you like to learn and practice your instrument alone or with a teacher or friend? If you sing, which kind of music do you gravitate toward? And if you could play *any* instrument, what would it be?

The twelve astrological signs we know today come from the twelve constellations arranged around the ecliptic of the sun's path. Astrologers observe these signs and interpret their effect on people and events. For example, an astrologer may note that as a Virgo, a person might be great at analysis but find it challenging to synthesize all the details. And a Scorpio may be drawn to jobs or a certain career where they can investigate people or subjects, but a corporate structure doesn't appeal to them. Through understanding your Sun sign, you have a unique window of insight into yourself and your life!

The prompts in this part will guide you through a deeper exploration of your Sun sign and the traits, relationship dynamics, and more that may be influenced by this sign. Reflect on how your career path may be impacted by your sign. Consider how a certain characteristic linked to your sign plays into how you handle conflict with friends. Through guided journaling, this part will help you get to know your-self better. Of course, there is much more to astrology than your personal Sun sign. If you are interested in knowing even more about your relationship with the cosmos, you can also look at the other signs in your birth chart, such as your ascendant sign. Or you may want to focus more deeply on general astrology, as well as your Sun sign and sign element, and revisit different prompts to see how your reflections may evolve. This is *your* astrological journey: Let it take you wher-ever you want to go!

# PART THREE

# GETTING TO KNOW YOUR SIGN

Pisces, the last sign of the zodiac, is often described as living between worlds. Their symbol is two fish bound together: one living in the depths of the ocean, the other above the seas. There is great sensitivity in this sign and a desire to turn away from tough real-world problems. Write about a time when you retreated and ignored the world's clamor for a time. Did you feel better after you emerged?

........................................................................................................
........................................................................................................
........................................................................................................
........................................................................................................
........................................................................................................
........................................................................................................
........................................................................................................
........................................................................................................
........................................................................................................
........................................................................................................
........................................................................................................
........................................................................................................
........................................................................................................
........................................................................................................
........................................................................................................
........................................................................................................
........................................................................................................
........................................................................................................
........................................................................................................
........................................................................................................
........................................................................................................
........................................................................................................

In ancient times, Pisces was ruled by Jupiter, the great benefic planet; however, since the discovery of Neptune in 1846, Neptune has had dominion over this sign. Astrologers describe Neptune as foggy, idealistic, spiritual, and, at many times, confused. Both Jupiter and Neptune energy can help Pisces with imaginative creations. Do you feel you are creative? In what ways? Write about a creative experience that seemed to happen effortlessly.

........................................................................................
........................................................................................
........................................................................................
........................................................................................
........................................................................................
........................................................................................
........................................................................................
........................................................................................
........................................................................................
........................................................................................
........................................................................................
........................................................................................
........................................................................................
........................................................................................
........................................................................................
........................................................................................
........................................................................................
........................................................................................
........................................................................................
........................................................................................
........................................................................................
........................................................................................

Of all the water element signs, Pisces is the slipperiest, meaning the hardest to pin to one characteristic or another. Your sign can be a shapeshifter and play many roles. Describe some of the different roles you may have played in your life. Which ones are the most effective and comfortable for you?

. . . . . . . . . . . . . . . . . . . . . . . . . . . . . . . . . . . . . . . . . . . . . . . . . . . . . . . . . . . . . . . . . . . . . . . . . . . . . . . . . . . . . . . . . . . . . . . . . . .

. . . . . . . . . . . . . . . . . . . . . . . . . . . . . . . . . . . . . . . . . . . . . . . . . . . . . . . . . . . . . . . . . . . . . . . . . . . . . . . . . . . . . . . . . . . . . . . . . . .

. . . . . . . . . . . . . . . . . . . . . . . . . . . . . . . . . . . . . . . . . . . . . . . . . . . . . . . . . . . . . . . . . . . . . . . . . . . . . . . . . . . . . . . . . . . . . . . . . . .

. . . . . . . . . . . . . . . . . . . . . . . . . . . . . . . . . . . . . . . . . . . . . . . . . . . . . . . . . . . . . . . . . . . . . . . . . . . . . . . . . . . . . . . . . . . . . . . . . . .

. . . . . . . . . . . . . . . . . . . . . . . . . . . . . . . . . . . . . . . . . . . . . . . . . . . . . . . . . . . . . . . . . . . . . . . . . . . . . . . . . . . . . . . . . . . . . . . . . . .

. . . . . . . . . . . . . . . . . . . . . . . . . . . . . . . . . . . . . . . . . . . . . . . . . . . . . . . . . . . . . . . . . . . . . . . . . . . . . . . . . . . . . . . . . . . . . . . . . . .

. . . . . . . . . . . . . . . . . . . . . . . . . . . . . . . . . . . . . . . . . . . . . . . . . . . . . . . . . . . . . . . . . . . . . . . . . . . . . . . . . . . . . . . . . . . . . . . . . . .

. . . . . . . . . . . . . . . . . . . . . . . . . . . . . . . . . . . . . . . . . . . . . . . . . . . . . . . . . . . . . . . . . . . . . . . . . . . . . . . . . . . . . . . . . . . . . . . . . . .

. . . . . . . . . . . . . . . . . . . . . . . . . . . . . . . . . . . . . . . . . . . . . . . . . . . . . . . . . . . . . . . . . . . . . . . . . . . . . . . . . . . . . . . . . . . . . . . . . . .

. . . . . . . . . . . . . . . . . . . . . . . . . . . . . . . . . . . . . . . . . . . . . . . . . . . . . . . . . . . . . . . . . . . . . . . . . . . . . . . . . . . . . . . . . . . . . . . . . . .

. . . . . . . . . . . . . . . . . . . . . . . . . . . . . . . . . . . . . . . . . . . . . . . . . . . . . . . . . . . . . . . . . . . . . . . . . . . . . . . . . . . . . . . . . . . . . . . . . . .

. . . . . . . . . . . . . . . . . . . . . . . . . . . . . . . . . . . . . . . . . . . . . . . . . . . . . . . . . . . . . . . . . . . . . . . . . . . . . . . . . . . . . . . . . . . . . . . . . . .

. . . . . . . . . . . . . . . . . . . . . . . . . . . . . . . . . . . . . . . . . . . . . . . . . . . . . . . . . . . . . . . . . . . . . . . . . . . . . . . . . . . . . . . . . . . . . . . . . . .

. . . . . . . . . . . . . . . . . . . . . . . . . . . . . . . . . . . . . . . . . . . . . . . . . . . . . . . . . . . . . . . . . . . . . . . . . . . . . . . . . . . . . . . . . . . . . . . . . . .

. . . . . . . . . . . . . . . . . . . . . . . . . . . . . . . . . . . . . . . . . . . . . . . . . . . . . . . . . . . . . . . . . . . . . . . . . . . . . . . . . . . . . . . . . . . . . . . . . . .

. . . . . . . . . . . . . . . . . . . . . . . . . . . . . . . . . . . . . . . . . . . . . . . . . . . . . . . . . . . . . . . . . . . . . . . . . . . . . . . . . . . . . . . . . . . . . . . . . . .

. . . . . . . . . . . . . . . . . . . . . . . . . . . . . . . . . . . . . . . . . . . . . . . . . . . . . . . . . . . . . . . . . . . . . . . . . . . . . . . . . . . . . . . . . . . . . . . . . . .

. . . . . . . . . . . . . . . . . . . . . . . . . . . . . . . . . . . . . . . . . . . . . . . . . . . . . . . . . . . . . . . . . . . . . . . . . . . . . . . . . . . . . . . . . . . . . . . . . . .

. . . . . . . . . . . . . . . . . . . . . . . . . . . . . . . . . . . . . . . . . . . . . . . . . . . . . . . . . . . . . . . . . . . . . . . . . . . . . . . . . . . . . . . . . . . . . . . . . . .

. . . . . . . . . . . . . . . . . . . . . . . . . . . . . . . . . . . . . . . . . . . . . . . . . . . . . . . . . . . . . . . . . . . . . . . . . . . . . . . . . . . . . . . . . . . . . . . . . . .

. . . . . . . . . . . . . . . . . . . . . . . . . . . . . . . . . . . . . . . . . . . . . . . . . . . . . . . . . . . . . . . . . . . . . . . . . . . . . . . . . . . . . . . . . . . . . . . . . . .

. . . . . . . . . . . . . . . . . . . . . . . . . . . . . . . . . . . . . . . . . . . . . . . . . . . . . . . . . . . . . . . . . . . . . . . . . . . . . . . . . . . . . . . . . . . . . . . . . . .

Pets and the animal kingdom are a comforting area for Pisces. The immediate emotional communication between you and your dog, horse, cat, or other beloved animal feels pure and warm. No confusing words or intentions here! Describe your relationship with pets and animals in general. What do you value most about these bonds?

.................................................................................
.................................................................................
.................................................................................
.................................................................................
.................................................................................
.................................................................................
.................................................................................
.................................................................................
.................................................................................
.................................................................................
.................................................................................
.................................................................................
.................................................................................
.................................................................................
.................................................................................
.................................................................................
.................................................................................
.................................................................................
.................................................................................
.................................................................................
.................................................................................
.................................................................................
.................................................................................

........................................................................................

........................................................................................

........................................................................................

........................................................................................

........................................................................................

........................................................................................

........................................................................................

........................................................................................

........................................................................................

........................................................................................

........................................................................................

........................................................................................

........................................................................................

........................................................................................

........................................................................................

........................................................................................

........................................................................................

........................................................................................

........................................................................................

........................................................................................

........................................................................................

........................................................................................

........................................................................................

........................................................................................

........................................................................................

........................................................................................

........................................................................................

........................................................................................

........................................................................................

........................................................................................

........................................................................................

........................................................................................

........................................................................................

Listening to music is often the best way for Pisces to surround themselves with good vibes. What is your favorite type of music? Have you ever thought of music as medicine to calm or enliven your mood? Describe your playlist for relaxing, getting your energy up, or inspiring you.

.........................................................................................
.........................................................................................
.........................................................................................
.........................................................................................
.........................................................................................
.........................................................................................
.........................................................................................
.........................................................................................
.........................................................................................
.........................................................................................
.........................................................................................
.........................................................................................
.........................................................................................
.........................................................................................
.........................................................................................
.........................................................................................
.........................................................................................
.........................................................................................
.........................................................................................
.........................................................................................
.........................................................................................
.........................................................................................
.........................................................................................
.........................................................................................

Pisces rules the feet, the part of the body that attaches you to the earth. And good shoes are essential to keeping your feet protected and content. Are you a shoe person? Do you go to great lengths to find attractive but comfortable shoes? Write about your relationship with shoes and how you feel about various kinds of shoes.

Pisces is a mystical sign in the sense that she is attuned to unseen vibrations and easily senses connections in a relationship and how they might develop in the future. Have your presentiments worked out so far?

..................................................................................................
..................................................................................................
..................................................................................................
..................................................................................................
..................................................................................................
..................................................................................................
..................................................................................................
..................................................................................................
..................................................................................................
..................................................................................................
..................................................................................................
..................................................................................................
..................................................................................................
..................................................................................................
..................................................................................................
..................................................................................................
..................................................................................................
..................................................................................................
..................................................................................................
..................................................................................................
..................................................................................................
..................................................................................................
..................................................................................................
..................................................................................................
..................................................................................................

Pisces likes to live in sight of a body of water. What body of water do you feel most comfortable near or in: ocean, lake, pond, calm sea, rapids, or even a small puddle? Write about your relationship to bodies of water and any of your experiences in them.

Falling asleep can sometimes be difficult for Pisces, as it takes a while to calm down from all the vibrations of the day. What do you do to promote sleep? Are you mindful of closing all electronics at least an hour before bed? Describe your nighttime ritual.

The energy of Pisces' ruling planet, Neptune, can promote illusions and flights of fancy that aren't based in reality. Write about a time when your ideas or wishes took over regardless of their practicality or "do-ability."

Soft fabric comforts and cuddles Pisces. Which is your favorite? Silk, chenille, jersey, cotton? Write about an article of clothing that always makes you feel good. What color is it? When do you wear it?

Neptune, your ruling planet, governs all spiritual practices, which can help you connect with your inner self. Do you meditate on colors, words, or melodies? What works best for you? Write about your experiences and feelings with this spiritual practice. If you are just beginning, write down your thoughts about why you want to start meditating.

........................................................................................................
........................................................................................................
........................................................................................................
........................................................................................................
........................................................................................................
........................................................................................................
........................................................................................................
........................................................................................................
........................................................................................................
........................................................................................................
........................................................................................................
........................................................................................................
........................................................................................................
........................................................................................................
........................................................................................................
........................................................................................................
........................................................................................................
........................................................................................................
........................................................................................................
........................................................................................................
........................................................................................................
........................................................................................................
........................................................................................................
........................................................................................................

Mystical feelings can come through dreams, and Pisces often is a true dreamer—meaning that your dreams can reveal truths about yourself, other people, or even events. Do you keep a dream journal? It is often a good idea for Pisces. Write about a particularly memorable dream. Were there certain colors in it? Water? Animals?

..........................................................................................
..........................................................................................
..........................................................................................
..........................................................................................
..........................................................................................
..........................................................................................
..........................................................................................
..........................................................................................
..........................................................................................
..........................................................................................
..........................................................................................
..........................................................................................
..........................................................................................
..........................................................................................
..........................................................................................
..........................................................................................
..........................................................................................
..........................................................................................
..........................................................................................
..........................................................................................
..........................................................................................
..........................................................................................
..........................................................................................

Neptune, Pisces' ruling planet, also rules orchids and African violets. These plants can be tricky to cultivate, but their colors are Piscean favorites! Write about any feelings and/or experiences you have had with these beautiful flowers.

.............................................................................................

.............................................................................................

.............................................................................................

.............................................................................................

.............................................................................................

.............................................................................................

.............................................................................................

.............................................................................................

.............................................................................................

.............................................................................................

.............................................................................................

.............................................................................................

.............................................................................................

.............................................................................................

.............................................................................................

.............................................................................................

.............................................................................................

.............................................................................................

.............................................................................................

.............................................................................................

.............................................................................................

.............................................................................................

.............................................................................................

.............................................................................................

.............................................................................................

Many people believe that we have lived in times past, and these past lives can influence our present lifetime. Pisces, being sensitive to all unseen vibrations, may recall a past historical period when she lived. If this describes you, when was this life and where? Who were you at that time? If you could choose a past life, what would it be? Do you believe it is useful to understand past lives? Have you ever felt that something from a past life influences your current life?

..................................................................................................
..................................................................................................
..................................................................................................
..................................................................................................
..................................................................................................
..................................................................................................
..................................................................................................
..................................................................................................
..................................................................................................
..................................................................................................
..................................................................................................
..................................................................................................
..................................................................................................
..................................................................................................
..................................................................................................
..................................................................................................
..................................................................................................
..................................................................................................
..................................................................................................
..................................................................................................
..................................................................................................

The gem amethyst is often a Pisces favorite. Holding this beautiful purple stone in your left hand (the receptive side of the body) can enhance meditation and calming thoughts. Also, soaking amethyst in spring water, leaving it in the sun, and then drinking the water bring the amethyst vibrations into your body. Try keeping amethyst close for a week. Then describe your feelings or any experiences with this gem.

Exercise may not be your favorite activity. Pisces likes to flow along with life rather than be energized with pumping cardio. But there are many exercises that help you flow. Aikido is a gentle martial art. And for a beautiful example of flowing energy, take a look at Pisces and Olympic gold medal winner Simone Biles. Her gymnastics are inspiring. What exercise do you enjoy?

........................................................................................................

........................................................................................................

........................................................................................................

........................................................................................................

........................................................................................................

........................................................................................................

........................................................................................................

........................................................................................................

........................................................................................................

........................................................................................................

........................................................................................................

........................................................................................................

........................................................................................................

........................................................................................................

........................................................................................................

........................................................................................................

........................................................................................................

........................................................................................................

........................................................................................................

........................................................................................................

........................................................................................................

........................................................................................................

Cushy pillows on your bed and perhaps special stuffed animals help Pisces relax. Do you decorate with soft pillows? Write about how you feel as you sink into your favorite comforter or pillow for a nap or when going to bed for the night.

Each zodiac sign has a shadow side that challenges the personality. For Pisces, their innate sensitivity can lead to overeating or using prescription drugs or alcohol to avoid facing difficulties. Write about how you soothe yourself. Do you tend to eat when feeling upset or overwhelmed? Are drugs and/or alcohol an escape for you?

Pisces is usually very compassionate with friends and relatives but doesn't always show the same consideration to herself. Write about a time when you forgave yourself for your actions. How did you feel? Exploring more self-compassion, in addition to being an important part of taking care of yourself, can also help combat overindulgence or unhealthy outlets for self-soothing.

. . . . . . . . . . . . . . . . . . . . . . . . . . . . . . . . . . . . . . . . . . . . . . . . . . . . . . . . . . . . . . . . . . . . . . . . . . . . . . . . . . . . . .

. . . . . . . . . . . . . . . . . . . . . . . . . . . . . . . . . . . . . . . . . . . . . . . . . . . . . . . . . . . . . . . . . . . . . . . . . . . . . . . . . . . . . .

. . . . . . . . . . . . . . . . . . . . . . . . . . . . . . . . . . . . . . . . . . . . . . . . . . . . . . . . . . . . . . . . . . . . . . . . . . . . . . . . . . . . . .

. . . . . . . . . . . . . . . . . . . . . . . . . . . . . . . . . . . . . . . . . . . . . . . . . . . . . . . . . . . . . . . . . . . . . . . . . . . . . . . . . . . . . .

. . . . . . . . . . . . . . . . . . . . . . . . . . . . . . . . . . . . . . . . . . . . . . . . . . . . . . . . . . . . . . . . . . . . . . . . . . . . . . . . . . . . . .

. . . . . . . . . . . . . . . . . . . . . . . . . . . . . . . . . . . . . . . . . . . . . . . . . . . . . . . . . . . . . . . . . . . . . . . . . . . . . . . . . . . . . .

. . . . . . . . . . . . . . . . . . . . . . . . . . . . . . . . . . . . . . . . . . . . . . . . . . . . . . . . . . . . . . . . . . . . . . . . . . . . . . . . . . . . . .

. . . . . . . . . . . . . . . . . . . . . . . . . . . . . . . . . . . . . . . . . . . . . . . . . . . . . . . . . . . . . . . . . . . . . . . . . . . . . . . . . . . . . .

. . . . . . . . . . . . . . . . . . . . . . . . . . . . . . . . . . . . . . . . . . . . . . . . . . . . . . . . . . . . . . . . . . . . . . . . . . . . . . . . . . . . . .

. . . . . . . . . . . . . . . . . . . . . . . . . . . . . . . . . . . . . . . . . . . . . . . . . . . . . . . . . . . . . . . . . . . . . . . . . . . . . . . . . . . . . .

. . . . . . . . . . . . . . . . . . . . . . . . . . . . . . . . . . . . . . . . . . . . . . . . . . . . . . . . . . . . . . . . . . . . . . . . . . . . . . . . . . . . . .

. . . . . . . . . . . . . . . . . . . . . . . . . . . . . . . . . . . . . . . . . . . . . . . . . . . . . . . . . . . . . . . . . . . . . . . . . . . . . . . . . . . . . .

. . . . . . . . . . . . . . . . . . . . . . . . . . . . . . . . . . . . . . . . . . . . . . . . . . . . . . . . . . . . . . . . . . . . . . . . . . . . . . . . . . . . . .

. . . . . . . . . . . . . . . . . . . . . . . . . . . . . . . . . . . . . . . . . . . . . . . . . . . . . . . . . . . . . . . . . . . . . . . . . . . . . . . . . . . . . .

. . . . . . . . . . . . . . . . . . . . . . . . . . . . . . . . . . . . . . . . . . . . . . . . . . . . . . . . . . . . . . . . . . . . . . . . . . . . . . . . . . . . . .

. . . . . . . . . . . . . . . . . . . . . . . . . . . . . . . . . . . . . . . . . . . . . . . . . . . . . . . . . . . . . . . . . . . . . . . . . . . . . . . . . . . . . .

. . . . . . . . . . . . . . . . . . . . . . . . . . . . . . . . . . . . . . . . . . . . . . . . . . . . . . . . . . . . . . . . . . . . . . . . . . . . . . . . . . . . . .

. . . . . . . . . . . . . . . . . . . . . . . . . . . . . . . . . . . . . . . . . . . . . . . . . . . . . . . . . . . . . . . . . . . . . . . . . . . . . . . . . . . . . .

. . . . . . . . . . . . . . . . . . . . . . . . . . . . . . . . . . . . . . . . . . . . . . . . . . . . . . . . . . . . . . . . . . . . . . . . . . . . . . . . . . . . . .

. . . . . . . . . . . . . . . . . . . . . . . . . . . . . . . . . . . . . . . . . . . . . . . . . . . . . . . . . . . . . . . . . . . . . . . . . . . . . . . . . . . . . .

. . . . . . . . . . . . . . . . . . . . . . . . . . . . . . . . . . . . . . . . . . . . . . . . . . . . . . . . . . . . . . . . . . . . . . . . . . . . . . . . . . . . . .

. . . . . . . . . . . . . . . . . . . . . . . . . . . . . . . . . . . . . . . . . . . . . . . . . . . . . . . . . . . . . . . . . . . . . . . . . . . . . . . . . . . . . .

There are many ways a sensitive Pisces can encourage Neptune's mystical and spiritual vibes. Crystal balls, tarot cards, or using a pendulum are a few techniques for channeling your intuition. Purchase one of these tools and start practicing. Record the answers you glean.

Diet is an area that Pisces sometimes forgets. Lost in your feelings, you may forget to eat or just grab a smoothie. Lack of nutrition lowers your energy and can lead to junk food cravings. Record your meals for a week or so. Do you see a pattern? Write about what you would like to change about your eating habits.

Pisces rules the feet. Have you ever had a reflexology treatment? This is a special massage for feet that stimulates or calms the acupuncture meridians of the entire body. A foot rub from a friend or partner can also be soothing. Give either of these practices a try and write about your experience.

........................................................................
........................................................................
........................................................................
........................................................................
........................................................................
........................................................................
........................................................................
........................................................................
........................................................................
........................................................................
........................................................................
........................................................................
........................................................................
........................................................................
........................................................................
........................................................................
........................................................................
........................................................................
........................................................................
........................................................................
........................................................................
........................................................................
........................................................................

Some of the greatest dancers in the world have been Pisces! Dancing is a form of expression that comes naturally to many Pisces. Ballet, hip-hop, modern, tango, jazz, ballroom: Whatever type of dance you like, write about your experiences. Or, how do you imagine dancing with a special partner?

........................................................................................................

........................................................................................................

........................................................................................................

........................................................................................................

........................................................................................................

........................................................................................................

........................................................................................................

........................................................................................................

........................................................................................................

........................................................................................................

........................................................................................................

........................................................................................................

........................................................................................................

........................................................................................................

........................................................................................................

........................................................................................................

........................................................................................................

........................................................................................................

........................................................................................................

........................................................................................................

........................................................................................................

........................................................................................................

........................................................................................................

........................................................................................................

........................................................................................................

Pisces is a mutable sign, meaning she bridges the gap between seasons (in this case, winter and spring). All mutable signs are adaptable and flexible, and Pisces as a mutable water sign is fluid and changeable with her feelings. Write about a time when you were so flexible in a relationship that it brought confusion. Or a time when your intuitions effortlessly helped you flow into a solution.

........................................................................................................
........................................................................................................
........................................................................................................
........................................................................................................
........................................................................................................
........................................................................................................
........................................................................................................
........................................................................................................
........................................................................................................
........................................................................................................
........................................................................................................
........................................................................................................
........................................................................................................
........................................................................................................
........................................................................................................
........................................................................................................
........................................................................................................
........................................................................................................
........................................................................................................
........................................................................................................
........................................................................................................
........................................................................................................
........................................................................................................
........................................................................................................
........................................................................................................
........................................................................................................
........................................................................................................
........................................................................................................

Film and photography, which capture beautiful moments or natural beauty, are wonderful activities for Pisces to explore the world through. Sometimes pictures communicate more than words for Pisces. *Instagram* sharing is tailor-made for your sign! Imagine compiling a Piscean *Instagram* account or set of posts during your birth month. Plan it out in this journal.

.....................................................................................................................
.....................................................................................................................
.....................................................................................................................
.....................................................................................................................
.....................................................................................................................
.....................................................................................................................
.....................................................................................................................
.....................................................................................................................
.....................................................................................................................
.....................................................................................................................
.....................................................................................................................
.....................................................................................................................
.....................................................................................................................
.....................................................................................................................
.....................................................................................................................
.....................................................................................................................
.....................................................................................................................
.....................................................................................................................
.....................................................................................................................
.....................................................................................................................
.....................................................................................................................
.....................................................................................................................
.....................................................................................................................
.....................................................................................................................
.....................................................................................................................

# ADDITIONAL RESOURCES

**Websites and Other Digital Resources**

www.alabe.com

www.astro.com

www.astrodienst.com

www.lunarium.co.uk

www.changingofthegods.com

App: Co-Star

**Books**

*Astrology, Psychology and the Four Elements* by Stephen Arroyo

*The Astrology of Fate* by Liz Greene

*Sun Signs* by Linda Goodman

*Relationship Signs* by Linda Goodman

*If You Want to Write* by Brenda Ueland

*The Artist's Way* by Julia Cameron

*The Hidden Life of Trees* by Peter Wohlleben

*The Hidden Power of Everyday Things* by Constance Stellas, Julie Gillentine, and Jonathan Sharp

*Sex Signs* by Constance Stellas

*The Astrological Guide to Self-Care* by Constance Stellas

*How to Be an Astrologer* by Constance Stellas

*The Little Book of Self-Care* by Constance Stellas

# BIBLIOGRAPHY

Arroyo, Stephen. *Astrology, Psychology and the Four Elements.* Davis, CA: CRCS, 1975.

Arroyo, Stephen. *Relationships & Life Cycles.* Vancouver, WA: CRCS, 1979.

Donath, Emma Belle. *Have We Met Before?* Tempe, AZ: American Federation of Astrologers, 1982.

Forrest, Steven. *The Book of Neptune.* Borrego Springs, CA: Seven Paws, 2016.

Forrest, Steven. *The Book of Fire.* Borrego Springs, CA: Seven Paws, 2019.

Green, Jeffrey Wolf. *Pluto: The Evolutionary Journey of the Soul, Volume I.* St. Paul, MN: Llewellyn, 1985.

Green, Jeffrey Wolf. *Pluto: The Soul's Evolution Through Relationships, Volume II.* St. Paul, MN: Llewellyn, 1997.

Greene, Liz. *The Astrology of Fate.* York Beach, ME: Weiser, 1984.

Hickey, Isabel M. *Astrology: A Cosmic Science.* Sebastopol, CA: CRCS, 2011.

Oken, Alan. *Soul Centered Astrology.* New York: Bantam, 1990.

Sargent, Lois Haines. *How to Handle Your Human Relations.* Tempe, AZ: American Federation of Astrologers, 1958.

Tester, Jim. *A History of Western Astrology.* New York: Ballantine, 1987.

Yott, Donald H. *Astrology and Reincarnation.* York Beach, ME: Weiser, 1989.

# DEDICATION

To all those seeking the wisdom in their stars.

# ACKNOWLEDGMENTS

I would like to thank Karen Cooper and everyone at Adams Media who helped with this book. To Brendan O'Neill, Katie Corcoran Lytle, Laura Daly, Julia Jacques, Sarah Doughty, Jo-Anne Duhamel, Julia DeGraf, and everyone else who worked on the manuscripts. To Frank Rivera, Priscilla Yuen, Colleen Cunningham, and Tess Armstrong for their work on the book's cover and interior design. I appreciated your team spirit and eagerness to dive into the riches of astrology.

# Unique ways to
# refresh and restore—
# personalized for your
# ZODIAC SIGN!

## PICK UP OR DOWNLOAD YOUR COPIES TODAY!